# DOODLE YOUR
# WORRIES AWAY

also in the *CBT Doodling* series

**CBT Doodling for Kids**
50 Illustrated Handouts to Help Build Confidence
and Emotional Resilience in Children Aged 6–11
*Tanja Sharpe*
ISBN 978 1 78592 537 5


of related interest

**The Healthy Coping Colouring Book and Journal**
Creative Activities to Help Manage Stress,
Anxiety and Other Big Feelings
*Pooky Knightsmith*
*Illustrated by Emily Hamilton*
ISBN 978 1 78592 139 1
eISBN 978 1 78450 405 2


**The Can-Do Kid's Journal**
Discover Your Confidence Superpower!
*Sue Atkins*
*Illustrated by Amy Bradley*
ISBN 978 1 78775 271 9
eISBN 978 1 78775 272 6


**Binnie the Baboon Anxiety and Stress Activity Book**
A Therapeutic Story with Creative and CBT Activities
To Help Children Aged 5–10 Who Worry
*Dr Karen Treisman*
*Illustrated by Sarah Peacock*
ISBN 978 1 78592 554 2
eISBN 978 1 78775 200 9

# DOODLE YOUR WORRIES AWAY

A CBT Doodling Workbook for Children
Who Feel Worried or Anxious

## TANJA SHARPE

**Jessica Kingsley Publishers**
London and Philadelphia

First published in Great Britain in 2022 by Jessica Kingsley Publishers
An Hachette Company

1

Copyright © Tanja Sharpe 2022
Foreword copyright © Suzanne Alderson 2022

A CIP catalogue record for this title is available from the British Library and the Library of Congress

ISBN 978 1 78775 790 5
eISBN 978 1 78775 791 2

Printed and bound in Great Britain by Bell & Bain Limited

Jessica Kingsley Publishers' policy is to use papers that are natural, renewable and recyclable
products and made from wood grown in sustainable forests. The logging and manufacturing
processes are expected to conform to the environmental regulations of the country of origin.

Jessica Kingsley Publishers
Carmelite House
50 Victoria Embankment
London EC4Y 0DZ

www.jkp.com

# CONTENTS

# FOREWORD

The last time I remember consciously doodling – before I met Tanja – was circa 1985. Sitting next to the window in my least favourite class, with a head full of teenage angst, life trauma and unreleased emotion, I was struck by the beauty of the clouds passing by. In fact, I was mesmerized. As the teacher called my name insistently for the third or fourth time, I forced my eyes away to concentrate on the algebra challenge on the board. But instead of focusing on exponents and variables, I found my pen traversing the pages of my exercise book with a dotty, stripy, swirly recreation of the voluminous calm I'd seen through the window.

This wasn't the first time I had doodled; most of my school books were embellished with them. And, at the time, I saw them as a manifestation of ennui; an involuntary motion that my brain demanded as an escape from my conscious thoughts. Or indeed, Maths. No-one, especially not my teachers, seemed to appreciate what went into them or what came out of them, including me at the time. And so doodling became something I weaned myself off. It didn't seem to have a place in the adult world.

Doodling has been seen as a sign of a distracted mind or boredom, or a waste of productive time, but studies have shown that it improves concentration and recall and lowers our anxiety levels. Doodling stimulates the brain in so many ways, allowing us to retain more information than non-doodlers, stimulating blood flow to the pre-frontal cortex (the reward part of the brain) increasing feelings of creativity and problem solving skills, and reducing cortisol, the stress hormone.

It wasn't until I met Tanja Sharpe, in 2018, that I saw its power in action. I noticed that her messages were embellished with the most beautiful doodles, not always drawn by hand, sometimes with digital emojis and hearts. As we became firm friends and explored how the work we do – Tanja at Creative Counsellors and me at Parenting Mental Health – might come together, I noticed that Tanja always included her own form of notation for everything she wrote. The simple act of underlining – beautifully – or creating intricate corners for a page was a part of her thought process. It didn't diminish her ideas; it gave them space to form without constraint. It anchored her in her creativity and it made a thought into a 'thing'. It gave them strength and power.

And that is what doodling does. It switches off the conscious part of the brain so that we can allow ourselves to hear what our bodies and minds are saying. When we don't have a language to share our feelings and emotions, doodling can be a short cut to understanding and self-expression. It can help with emotional release and regulation. It can bring us calm.

The act of doodling encourages curiosity – in what we might create, what we might be thinking, what we might be feeling. And it creates a space where our state of 'being' speaks, rather than our state of 'doing'. An infinite game, where no-one wins or loses, it gives us permission to feel however we feel and to express it however we need to. It can be a release from having to find the words, yet enable as powerful a realization as if we had written an essay.

Tanja recently ran a series of workshops for the parents of young people with mental health issues who we support at Parenting Mental Health and doodling was at its core. After just the first session, parents were sharing that they felt lighter, more creative and were judging themselves less. They were more in tune with their emotions and less quick to diminish their feelings.

While you may have picked this book up for your child or one you are working with, I encourage you to approach the pages for your own self-discovery too. The themes within it are universal. And unlike so much of life, a doodle is exactly what it needs to be, however it comes out. By allowing ourselves to be okay with whatever appears, we can gift ourselves a sense of compassion and completeness, however we are feeling.

I hope you can hear Tanja's warm voice encouraging you and your child to explore the pages ahead without judgement and that it sparks the kind of creativity and calm that Tanja embodies. And I hope you know that whatever emotion, stress or worry you or your child brings to it, it's okay. You really can't go wrong with a doodle.

*Suzanne Alderson, author, community builder*
*and leader, charity founder, doodler*

# INTRODUCTION FOR ADULTS

This creative CBT doodle therapy workbook is designed for counsellors, coaches, therapists, teachers, school staff, parents, carers and professionals who support young people aged 8+ to express their worries and anxieties. It has been designed in a way that young people are also able to explore themselves. We tackle common themes around worrying, with an aim to help young people to understand why we worry, how this affects us and what we can do about it. Taking inspiration from the CBT (Cognitive Behavioural Therapy) model and my bespoke Confident Hearts Creative Wellbeing & Mindfulness® coaching programme, I have developed a fun and engaging way to help young people 'express their stress' and tune into their ability to solve their own problems with a little guidance from the adults around them. I found that this was the best way to help young people to feel confident to find solutions to their own worries, and this has formed the foundation for the way that I teach and have coached since 2015. I have been successfully coaching, mentoring and teaching other professionals to deliver my coaching programme globally, and have delivered thousands of hours of therapeutic support. All these worksheets aim to empower young people with the knowledge and confidence to tackle their worries and build stronger resilience.

This workbook approaches anxiety and worrying from an integrative approach, offering advice on creative expression, doodling,

CBT tools, compassion and confidence building self-talk, as well as Mindfulness tools.

## Creative expression

Creativity plays a big role in how young people process their worries. This is a natural part of human development and young people problem solve through play, art, drama and doodling. When we are being creative, we relax our nervous system and give our minds a chance to check in with how we are feeling and thinking.

## Doodling

Doodling is mostly an unconscious act of expression. Our unconscious mind is the filing cabinet where we file away all our emotions, memories and experiences. These stay there mostly without us knowing until we need them. Sometimes our brains can be overactive and cause excessive worrying and anxiety. Doodling helps us to distract our minds to offer a break as well as releasing things that are being stored away that may be causing us to worry. It is also a great way to problem solve without even knowing it!

## CBT tools

The CBT model is one of the most recognized models to support young people to express and take charge of their anxiety or worrying. In this book, we merge CBT with other powerful tools in a way that helps young people to access confidence-boosting CBT tools in a creative and fun way. We explore how our thoughts, emotions, body and actions all affect our worries and how we can work with the cycle instead of fighting against it to help us to feel good and confident in dealing with our challenges and our worries.

```
        ┌─────────────────────┐
        │      Thoughts       │
        │  What we think affects  │
        │   how we act and feel   │
        └─────────────────────┘
```

```
┌──────────────────┐      ┌──────────────────┐
│     Actions      │      │     Emotions     │
│ What we do affects │      │  What emotions we  │
│ how we think and feel │    │ feel affects how we │
│                  │      │   feel in our body   │
└──────────────────┘      └──────────────────┘

        ┌─────────────────────┐
        │        Body         │
        │   What we feel in our   │
        │   body affects how      │
        │    we think and act     │
        └─────────────────────┘
```

## Compassion and confidence building self-talk

More and more young people are struggling with putting themselves down and using unhelpful self-talk which makes them feel worse. In this book, we encourage kind, compassionate, caring and uplifting self-talk so that young people can grow in confidence and learn to trust their resilient and amazing bodies to know what to do and how to do it. We look at boundaries and trust and choosing people who make us feel good. This has been shown in my therapy room to really help young people to take charge of making healthy choices and boosting self-esteem.

## Mindfulness tools

As a Mindfulness coach and teacher, I have now trained over 130 coaches globally to deliver my unique Confident Hearts Creative Youth Wellbeing & Mindfulness® coaching programme in schools, clubs and in one-to-one sessions with young people. I believe in the power of Mindfulness as a tool to help young people to stop and check in with what they are thinking, feeling, saying and doing in their everyday lives. When we notice, we can make a change. When we notice, we can grow and learn and build resilience.

## Focus on normalizing worrying

Many young people do not know that it is normal to worry and can feel ashamed or believe that there is something wrong with them! They often don't realize that everyone worries, and this book will remind them that worrying is a natural part of being human, having a body and a brain. Sometimes we need a little help to make sense of our worries, and this is where you come in!

## Talking to young people about why we worry

It can be useful to talk to young people about why we worry, sharing some statements like:

- We will all go through times when we worry more than others.

- Our brains are problem-solving machines and just like a computer troubleshooter, our brains will keep thinking of the thing that is worrying us until we can solve the worry or it's not important anymore.

- Sometimes we can worry about other people, and this is normal too.

- If someone we care about is worrying, then sometimes we can worry more than usual too.

- There are times in our lives when it's normal to worry more than other times, like starting a new school or feeling like we are not making friends.

- It's okay to worry.

- Worrying is the brain's way of trying to help.

## Tips to support a young person to talk

- Give the young person lots of space and choose the right time to ask questions. On the way home from school when they feel tired and confused may not be the right time. Letting them cool down, rest and reset before asking about their day may help.

- Sharing some of your own stories of times when you have worried can help to normalize their worries.

- Focus your talks at times when they are most likely to engage, such as walking the dog, in the therapy room or when they come to you. Use distraction tools like the creativity in this book to help break the ice and start the conversations.

- Avoid trying to sway the young person into thinking one way or another. The more empowered young people are to find their own solutions, the more resilient they will become.

## Guiding young people through these worksheets

As you flick through these sheets you will notice that they have been created in black ink with plenty of white space to explore. They are designed very minimally on purpose to engage young people to use their own imagination to complete the doodle. This is where the magic of this book is. In my years as a therapist and a youth coach, I have found that I only have to start the story and the doodle, and how a young person continues the doodle is what is most important. I have also included lots of elements, such as:

- Thought bubbles to inspire young people to share their thoughts.

- Stars to help empower young people to trust in their own beliefs (reach for the stars).

- Hearts to engage emotions and bring feelings into the doodle.

- Arrows to guide young people to take action.

As you work through these sheets, I invite you to be non-directive and allow the young person to take their time with the doodle. We all process and heal at our own pace, and allowing young people the time that they need is a key aspect of creative expression.

Young people who are learning to trust themselves may ask for guidance, and sometimes we can best support by helping the young person to answer their own questions, for example:

*Young person*: What should I put here?

*Adult*: What do you really want to put there? What does your heart want you to put there? I know you have a brilliant brain, so what does your brain think you could put there?

This will help to support the young person in beginning to connect with their own intuition, and the more we can do this, the more resilient we are!

Most importantly, I hope that you are able to build loving and nurturing bonds with the young person you are supporting with this book. My wish is to see young people thriving, with hearts full of self-compassion and resilience.

Much love

*Tanja Sharpe*

P.S. If you would like to train to inspire young minds in your community through our signature Confident Hearts Creative Youth Wellbeing & Mindfulness® coaching programme, you can visit my website here: www.confidentheartsclub.com

# Oodles of Doodles

## How to Doodle

In this doodle drawing you can see lots of different shapes and designs like clouds, stars, faces, squiggle lines, zigzags, dots, spots, fish, hearts, eggs and other shapes. Doodling is simply making shapes and marks all over the paper without thinking too much about it! As you work through this book, fill the sheets with colour, shapes, words, feelings and anything else that you want to! You might want to add words that you cut out from a magazine or pictures of your friends or family. This is your book to explore anything and everything that you want to and in your own way!

We all worry about things. It's your brain's job to help you to be safe and happy in the world, and sometimes it can also be too protective. When your brain is being a little too protective because it cares about you, it can sometimes feel like anxiety. When you feel anxious, you can have headaches, feel angry, sad, feel sick in your stomach, be more tired than usual or even have more energy than usual. You may have lots of worrying thoughts too. Worrying thoughts are how your brain and your body are trying to help you to solve your problem. The doodles in this book can help you to share what you are feeling and thinking about and find ways to solve your problems.

If it helps, you may want to talk to someone who can help you, like a teacher, a counsellor or an adult you trust.

This is your book and you can use it in any way that you like.

**1**

# Thoughts Are Like Clouds

Thoughts float in and out of our minds like clouds float by in the sky. Some scientists say that we have around 100,000 thoughts every day. That's a lot of thoughts! Sometimes our thoughts can be sad and heavy like a rain cloud and we need to cry them out. Sometimes our thoughts can be dreamy like soft clouds floating through stars. Sometimes our thoughts can be bright and full of ideas like clouds in the sunshine. Sometimes our thoughts can be angry like lightning and storm clouds. All of our thoughts are normal and are important. We all have thoughts and all thoughts come and go. No thoughts stay forever!

**ACTION**: Create a cloud in the space that shows how you are feeling and thinking right now. Complete the doodle with shapes, colours, feelings or anything else that you want to add.

# 2

# Untangles

When we are trying to solve our problems or our worries, our thoughts can sometimes feel like they are getting tangled up. This is because our thoughts are going round in circles in our heads, and because we have so many of them it can make us feel really tired and confused. We can help our brains to work out our problems by writing them down and looking at them. When we write or draw our problems on paper, it gives our brains a break from tangling our thoughts up in one big mess!

**ACTION**: Using these thought bubbles, doodle what you think about a lot. Do you want to add anything else to your doodle? What colours would you give your thoughts? What other words or shapes would your thoughts be?

**3**

# Dream Doodles

Sometimes the thoughts that we have in our heads in the day can also visit our dreams at night. Sometimes when we are trying to solve a problem that we are having, we can have really weird dreams, and some of these dreams might even worry us a little more than usual. This is because our brains are really good at trying to help us to solve our problems, so they keep bringing back our worries over and over until we can solve them.

**ACTION**: Are you having any weird dreams? Draw, write or doodle the last dream that you can remember.

# 4

# Your Body Worry Map

When you worry about things, your body can create different chemicals that move all around your body and change the way you feel. We can feel this in different places. Sometimes people say things like 'It feels like butterflies in my stomach' and other people might say 'I'm feeling really hot' or even 'I have a bad headache'. We are all unique and we all feel our worries in our bodies differently. This is called your 'body worry map'. When you know your body worry map you can start to find ways to relax more and help your body.

**ACTION**: Have you ever stopped to notice what's happening in your body while you are worrying? Take a moment to think about all the ways that you feel worries in your body. This doodle is showing us that it feels its worries in its heart and in its stomach. Just like a map, start to draw, doodle, colour, write or express yourself in any way that you would like to.

## 5

# Lightbulb Thoughts

Sometimes our thoughts can come on like a lightbulb and surprise us out of nowhere! Like when we get really nervous about something that we didn't expect to feel nervous about. This is because we have so many thoughts in a day (remember scientists say we have about 100,000!) and our minds can't pay attention to them all. When we get a thought in our head that worries us, we also get a feeling in our body that can feel like worrying, just like the 'body worry map' in our last doodle. So, we might not realize that we are having a worrying thought until it flashes up and surprises us in our mind or our body! Every time we have a worrying thought that then passes, we get stronger! Our brains learn new ways to think faster and our body can get stronger too, just like the flower growing in the lightbulb. We grow new strength from surprise thoughts and feelings.

**ACTION**: Keep doodling a garden in the lightbulb. Would you like to add any lightbulb thoughts that have surprised you today? Can you remember a time when you had a lightbulb thought?

**6**

# A Day in the Life of You

Sometimes our worries can be with us all day. Have you ever had a day like this? Maybe something happened in your day that caused you to worry. Maybe you don't feel so good. Maybe you had a great day and have lots of happy thoughts. It's normal to have moments in your day when you are happy and moments when you worry. This changes like the weather. One minute it can be sunny and the next rain clouds can appear from nowhere.

**ACTION**: This doodle is all about your day. Share what a day in your life is like. Imagine that someone wrote a newspaper about your day – what would we read on the front page?

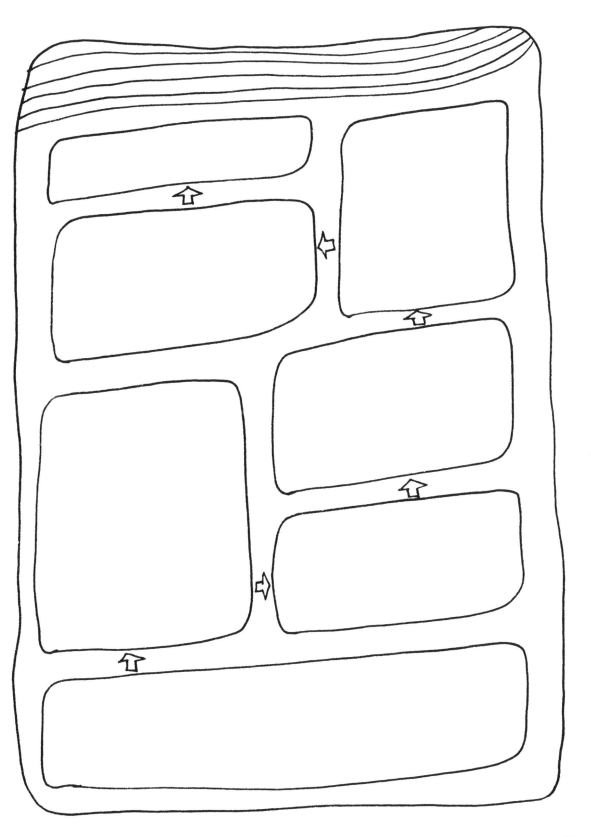

**7**

# Your Circle of Trust

Letting people into your 'circle of trust' is like giving someone an award for being awesome in your life. It is important to know who to have in your circle of trust and who might not be so trustworthy. How can you tell if you trust someone?

- Maybe you feel like you are safe with them.

- Maybe you feel happy when you spend time with them.

- They show you kindness.

- You know that you can ask them for help when you need it.

- They forgive you if you make a mistake (we all make mistakes, and it's one of the best ways to learn new stuff).

- You can share personal things with them.

**ACTION**: Who do you want to add to your 'circle of trust'? Who isn't in your 'circle of trust'? Doodle, paint, draw, add photos or anything that helps you to build your circle.

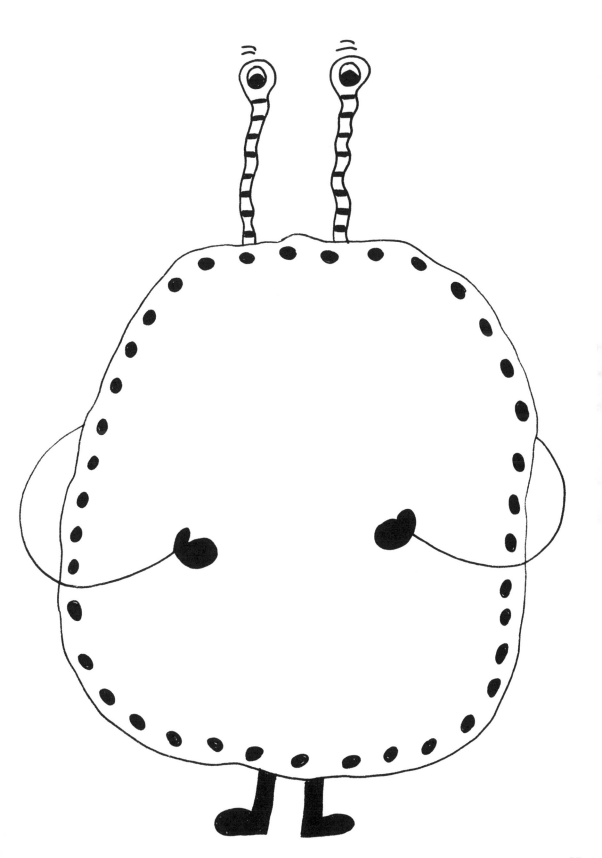

## 8

# Captain of Your Ship

Everyone will worry sometimes. Your body is designed to worry so you can look at your problems and find a way to solve them. Sometimes it can help to be the captain of your ship, and you can do this by imagining that you can sail above your worries, so high that when you are looking down you can focus on the worries that you want to. It sometimes helps to look at your worries from another angle. If you can see them in a different way, then you can also find a new way to solve them!

ACTION: Doodle all of the things that you are worrying about underneath the ship. Now imagine sailing high above them, so high that they don't feel so strong anymore while you are deciding what to do about them. You are the captain of your ship. You and your ship know where to go and what to do. As the captain of the ship where will you go first? Will you visit someone? Will you let go of a worry that you don't need to worry about anymore?

9

# Your Bag of Skills

Just like a magic bag of spells, there are lots of ways to help you to feel relaxed, even if you are worrying about something. The more relaxed you feel, the easier it is for you to find a way through your worries or to find a solution. It's easier to think of ways to feel good when you are not worrying. By doodling your bag of skills now, you will know how to help yourself to relax the next time you need it! Thinking about the different ways that help you to feel good is a skill. Knowing how to take care of yourself when you are worrying is also a skill. The more skills you have in your bag, the stronger you will be.

**ACTION**: Doodle, paint, draw and create all of the things that you can do to help you to feel relaxed and well on the bag. You can add people, places, colours, music, pets, games and anything else that you want. Your brain will now remember this when you need it! JUST LIKE MAGIC!

# Defenders

Sometimes we worry about getting ill or about the people we love getting ill. It's normal to worry about the people we love and also to think about what it might be like to feel ill. Everyone worries about this sometimes, but every now and again we can worry about this a lot, and may even start to become really anxious about this. Sometimes feeling anxious also feels like being ill. This can be confusing for our bodies and our brains. But did you know that your body is an amazing healer? When your body gets ill, your defenders defend it with an army of healthy bacteria. Every time we get ill and then get better, we get stronger and our army of bacteria gets stronger too.

**ACTION**: Complete this doodle, creating an army of defenders, and adding any shapes any shapes, colours or anything else that you want to.

## 11

# Listening Stars

Sometimes one of the best ways to help us to solve our problems and make big worries small is to talk to someone who is a great listener. We call these 'listening stars'. Listening stars are the kind of people who you can talk to about anything. They are friendly and caring and support you. Often when you talk about a problem with a listening star in your life, you can feel lighter, and the worries that you thought were really big can feel smaller. Listening stars can be friends, family, teachers, counsellors, your pets or anyone who helps you to share what's on your mind! Who are the listening stars in your life?

**ACTION**: Add your listening stars to your doodle. What else would you like to add to your doodle? What colours, shapes, words or feelings? Would you like to add a photo of someone who is a listening star for you?

# 12

# Your Worry Dragon

We can feel lots of different emotions and feelings when we have worries on our minds. Sometimes when we get tired from all the thinking and feeling we can also get snappy or angry. There are lots of reasons that we can feel this way – sometimes because our bodies feel tired or maybe we feel like something isn't fair or even that people aren't listening to us. It's normal to get snappy sometimes. Sometimes we may say things that we don't mean or do things that we don't feel good about. In this doodle, the worry dragon is hiding under a blanket because it feels upset that it threw a fireball at someone when it didn't mean to!

**ACTION**: Doodle all of the ways that you show others you are feeling snappy. Doodle different ways you might be able to show others you are feeling snappy.

 13

# I Need Space

Sometimes our heads can feel so full and noisy that we just need some time to ourselves. It's normal to want some space to clear your head and do something that feels relaxing or different to worrying. Sometimes we may even just want time to think on our own. It can help to have a way to show people that you need some time alone.

**ACTION**: Finish this doodle door hanger with a message that lets people know what you need. Would you like to share this with anyone? Maybe you could add them to your doodle and create a real door hanger if it helps?

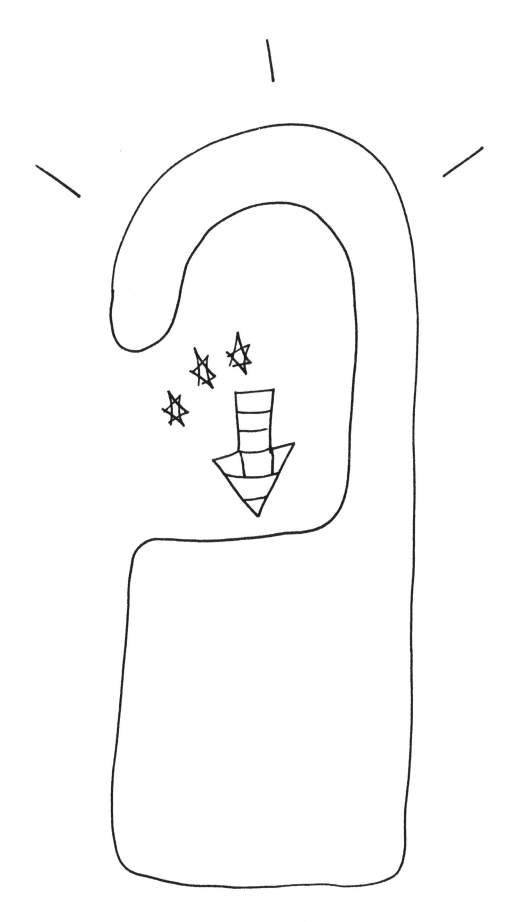

# 14

# Your Worry Iceberg

Have you ever seen an iceberg? Did you know that we only get to see the tip of the iceberg out of the water? Underneath is usually a much bigger hidden piece. This can be the same with our worries. We can often hide most of our worries away and only share little bits with others. Sometimes to solve a problem we need to look at the whole problem, with all of its worries. We need to see the whole iceberg to know how big it is. If we only look at a little bit of our worry, it may be harder to understand.

**ACTION**: Look at your whole worry like an iceberg. Add all of your thoughts and feelings to the doodle. Finish the doodle with shapes, colours and patterns. I wonder what you will create!

# 15

# Moodameleon

Did you know that scientists believe that chameleons can change their colours to show their moods? They have special cells called 'chromatophores' that can move around in their bodies when their mood changes. We show the world around us how we feel by our facial expressions and how we move our body. When someone is happy, they might smile, and their body might look relaxed. When someone is angry, they might clench their fists and frown. We show different emotions in different ways. We are all unique and we all express ourselves differently.

**ACTION**: Complete this doodle to show your mood right now. What colours show how you feel to others? What thoughts are you thinking? Do you want to add anything else to your doodle?

## 16

# Be a Unicorn Fish

Do you worry about what other people think of you? This is normal and one of the things that we can worry about the most. Some people believe that this is because of when we were cave people. When we were cave people it was safer to live in a tribe, and when we lived in a tribe there was always a leader who told everyone what to do. We didn't have houses with doors, and we didn't feel safe living alone with big woolly mammoths and cave bears around us. So we always needed a tribe of people to help collect firewood for the fire, to help bring food and to keep each other safe. We don't have to worry so much about this anymore as woolly mammoths aren't chasing us! We can be as unique as we want to be, and being unique means we can express ourselves with our clothes, our personality and our choices, just like a unicorn fish.

**ACTION**: Finish the doodle, adding colours, people, thoughts, words or anything else you want to add.

**17**

# My Big Jar of Love

What and who do you love? Love is an emotion that feels very different to anxiety, fear and worry. When we focus on love, we create a chemical reaction in our bodies that helps to send happy chemicals all around us. Think of someone or something that you love very much, someone or something that helps you to feel happy and relaxed. Does this feel different from worry or anxiety? How does this feel different?

**ACTION**: Add a heart for each pet, special place that you like to go to, songs, food that you like to eat, colours, people and anything else that you love. This jar is waiting for you to fill it with hearts. Don't forget to add yourself! Would you like someone else to help you to add hearts to your jar? When you need to, you can come back and remind yourself of all of these awesome things in your life!

## 18

# Your Power Shield

When we spend a lot of time worrying, we can easily forget all of the things that we are good at. The things we are good at are our superpowers. What superpowers do you have? Are you kind, a good friend, a brilliant listener? Are you fast at a sport, good at drawing or great at inventing things? What about other superpowers? If you could have any superpower in the world, what would you like to have and why?

**ACTION**: Add your superpowers to your power shield. Are there any colours or other doodles you would like to add? Remember that you can use these superpowers and your shield to remind yourself that you are awesome! What else can you use your shield for?

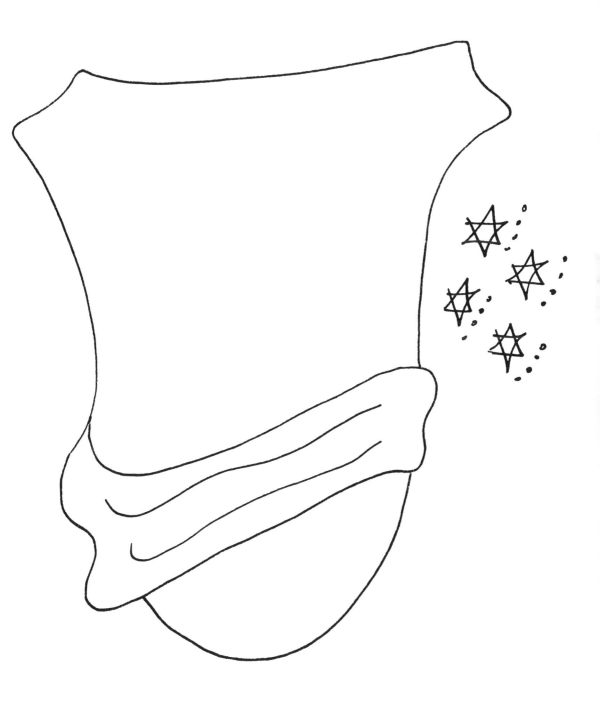

19

# Distraction Action

This doodle is called 'distraction action' because distraction can really help us when we are worrying. Taking some time out to do something creative helps to relax your brain and your body. If you can relax your brain and your body, then you may feel calmer and happier too. If you are focusing on this doodle, then it's much harder to focus on all of your worries too.

**ACTION**: Doodle colours, patterns and shapes in between the lines. Doodle your worries away.

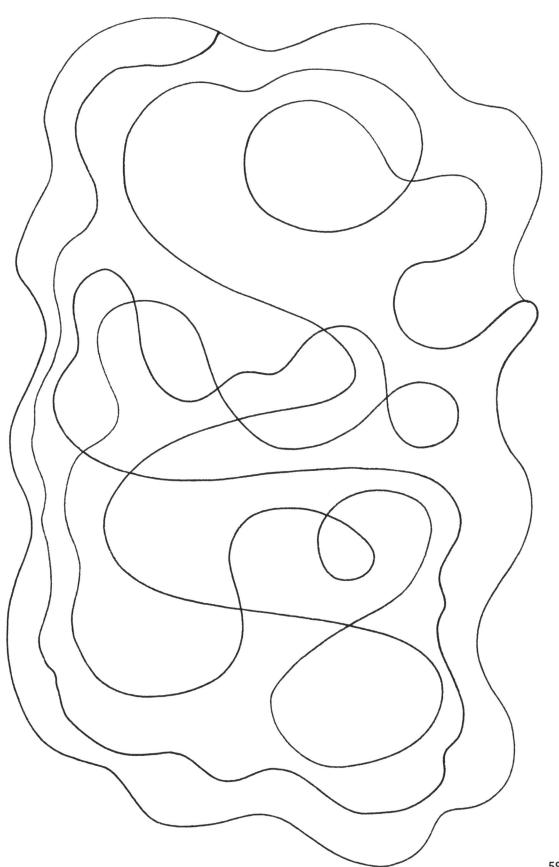

# 20

# A Big Page of Happy

Did you know that smiling is contagious, and sharing a smile when you are feeling troubled can help to change your mood? Scientists have actually studied smiling, and they found that when you smile, it changes how you feel. Isn't that a cool trick? The team on this page are your biggest supporters. They are here to cheer for you and spread a little happiness. They want you to know that whatever is going on for you now, and whatever worries you may have, they have a whole page of happy for you.

**ACTION**: Keep the 'big page of happy' growing, adding shapes and smiles and doodles until the whole page is filled. Keep this somewhere to remember that smiling is contagious.

## 21

# Octoloaded

Life can feel busy and sometimes we might wish that we had eight arms to handle everything that we need to do – homework, gaming, friends, exams and all the other things that can make us feel octoloaded. Sometimes taking a moment to write things down so that you can see what you need to do in front of you can help you to decide the most important things, kind of like making a 'to do' list. You may even realize that you didn't have as much to do as you thought you did! Or maybe you can work out what to do first so that you feel a little less worried.

**ACTION**: This doodle is a space for you to share the things that you need to do that are causing you to feel octoloaded and worried. Add your 'to do' list and any other doodles that you would like! Ask someone to help you if you need to talk about it.

63

## 22

# Mind Dump

Do you have someone on your mind you really want to say something to? Maybe you are worried about something and you want to say sorry? Maybe you want to let someone know how you are feeling but don't know how to say it? Writing your feelings and thoughts down to someone in a letter can help you to say the things that feel tricky to say out loud. It can feel really good to get something out of your head and onto paper, and this could help you to feel more confident to share your thoughts with someone else.

**ACTION**: Is there someone you want to write a message to? Practise here, and add anything else to the doodle that feels important to you.

## 23

# Mazed Out

Do you ever have those days when you feel like your thoughts are one big confusing mess? When you can't decide what to do or where to start? Sometimes we feel like a problem is so big that it will never go away or be fixed. The truth is that there are always lots of ways to solve problems, but sometimes we just can't find them easily. If we believe in ourselves and keep trying, we will find the solutions! Just like this maze!

**ACTION**: There is more than one way out of this maze! Can you find the different ways? Do you want to add anything else to this doodle? Maybe you could add the things you are trying to solve. Maybe you could add colours or patterns. You've got this!

## 24

# 'I Am' Reminders

It's normal to worry about something. We all do! Even though you are worrying, you are strong enough and will be okay. You have all the answers inside of you, although sometimes this might take a little time. Remember that each time you overcome a worry, you get stronger and quicker at helping yourself next time. It can help to doodle some notes to remind yourself that you are strong and amazing! Find somewhere to put these notes so you can see them when you are worrying. You could take a picture and save it on your phone. You could stick the notes on the back of your bedroom door so you see them when you wake up, or maybe you could stick them in your diary?

**ACTION**: Write three 'I am' reminders that help you to smile and feel strong inside. Start all your sentences with 'I am…' Keep doodling to cover this page with anything you like. The more you focus on them, the more you will start to feel and believe them!

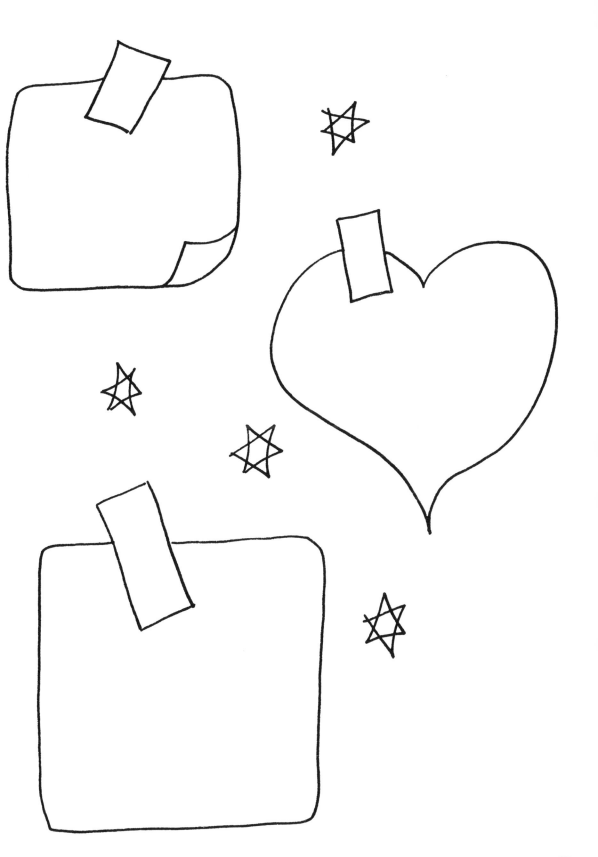

# 25

# Pots of What

People say that if we can find the end of the rainbow we will find a pot of gold. If you found a pot of gold, what would you do with it? Even better, what if we could find our own pots of something that had whatever we wanted most in them? What would that be like? If you found pots at the end of the rainbow, what would you love to be in them?

**ACTION**: Fill your pots with anything you like. You can doodle shapes, colours, words or anything else that you want to add. How would it feel to find these pots for real? Who would you share them with?

## 26

# Worry Stones

Some people believe that worry stones were first invented in Ancient Greece. All those years ago people would choose a stone and keep it with them. When they started to worry, they would pick up the stone and rub it between their fingers. This would help to create a relaxing feeling. Some people would also tell the stone their worries and then wash their worries away under water before going to bed. Sometimes it can be fun to collect your own stones and paint them with different doodle patterns. The next time you have a worry, you could find your stone and sit with it. Close your eyes, imagine your whole body relaxing and move your stone between your fingers.

**ACTION**: Would you like to create your first doodle worry stone pattern here? Draw random patterns, shapes, colours and doodles in these stones and create your own shape too. Would you like to add anything else?

## 27

# Take an Adventure

Using your imagination helps you to think creatively and differently. It can also help you to share your feelings and grow your problem-solving brain muscles. Imagine that this was a magic door and that by opening it you could create a whole new world of your own. What would your imaginary world look like? What would be in it? Who else would be there? Who wouldn't be there, and why? What colours would be in your world?

**ACTION**: Add colours, people, shapes, words or anything else you want to your doodle. What does it look like now?

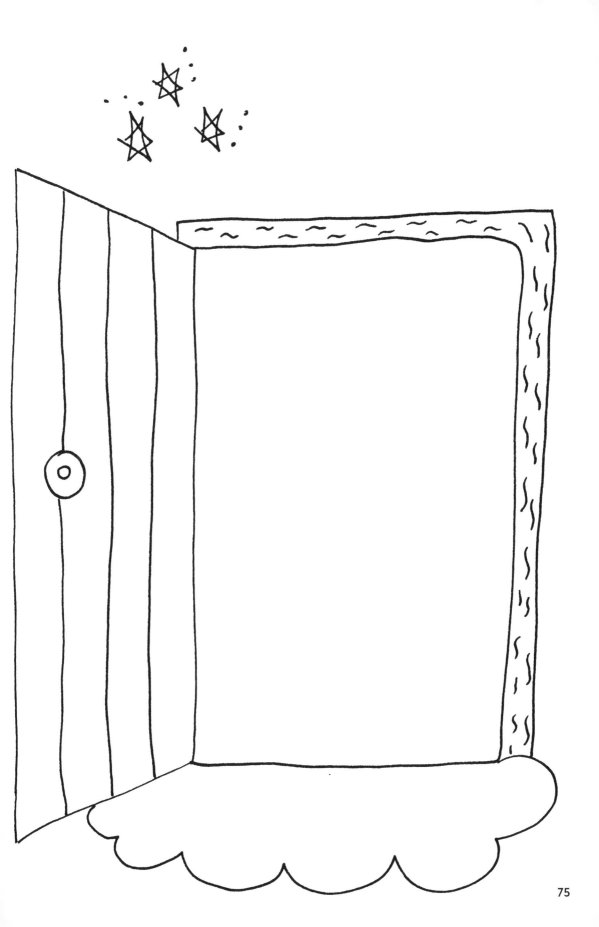

**28**

# What's Your Flavour?

We are all different in lots of different ways. Some of us have brown eyes and some of us have blue, green or mixed colour eyes. Some of us are taller than others. Some of us like the colour blue. Some of us eat spaghetti. Some of us like the beach. Some of us sing. Some of us have family who live in another country. Some of us wear jewellery. Some of us live in flats. Some of us have pets. Being different means that we have 'diversity'. Imagine if we were all the same – would that be so fun?

---

**ACTION**: If you were an ice cream, what flavour(s) and colour(s) would you be? We will all choose different colours and flavours. Has your flavour been invented yet? Invent a new colour and flavour to describe you. What other doodle patterns would be in your ice cream design? Celebrate how unique you are!

---

29

# Small Steps Are Big Steps

When we want to learn to bake a new cake, we need to know the recipe. Without the recipe we won't know what to buy or how long to cook the cake for. Sometimes when we want to do something new but don't have a plan or a recipe, we can spend a lot more time worrying about it. Is there something you want to do but you don't know how to do it? Maybe you want to learn something new or do well in an exam? Sometimes it can be hard to know where to start. Just like planning a recipe, these doodle steps are a great way to help you to get closer to what you want. When you have a plan, it's much easier to make it work.

**ACTION**: Write your goal in the cloud at the top and then write all of the steps that you can take to help you to reach your goal, kind of like a recipe. Doodle any other colours, shapes, words of encouragement or patterns onto your page. Where will you keep this to remind yourself of your plan?

 **30**

# Connected

Wi-Fi helps us to feel connected. We can go online and speak to someone in a different country. We can watch a film in another language. We can make new friends with people all over the world. Connected can be a feeling too. Who and what are you connected to most in this world, and why? What does being connected feel like to you?

**ACTION**: Add any people, places, pets or things that that you feel connected to in this doodle. What else do you feel connected to? What colours, patterns and shapes would you add?

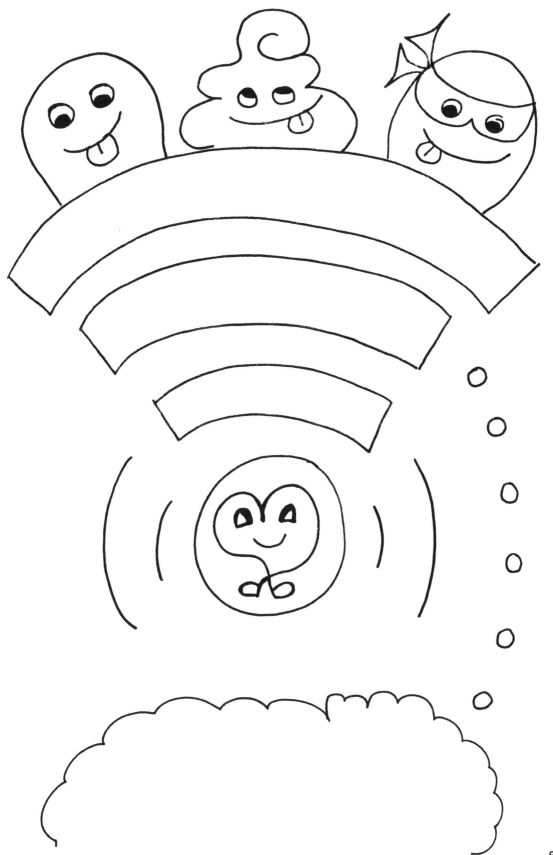

## 31

# Anchors

Anchors are things that help us to feel safe. Our brains like to feel safe, and when we feel safe, we don't worry so much. Just like a ship needs an anchor to keep it safe and still in the water, we also have anchors that help us. Anchors can be pets, people, toys, words, games, sayings and quotes, colours, smells and anything else that helps us to feel safe. Our anchors can also help us when we feel worried.

**ACTION**: Doodle all of the things, people, places and anything else that helps you to feel safe in this world. What other colours, patterns, places, people and doodles would you like to add to this?

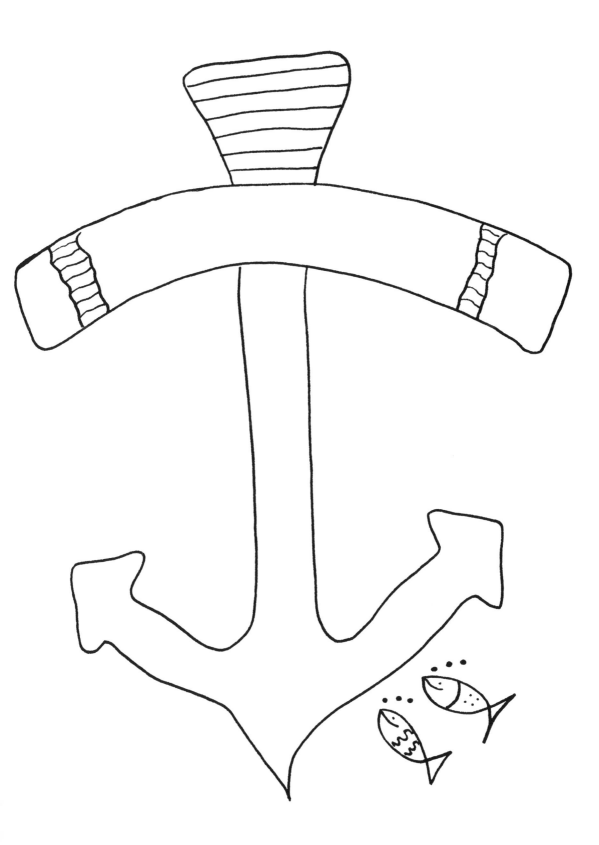

## 32

# Hideaway

Sometimes when we are worrying about something, our brains are working really hard to concentrate and we can become really sensitive or annoyed by other things like sounds, smells, colours and people. Sometimes we need to find somewhere to hide away for a moment and rest – like when you lie under your duvet or create a den in your house and hide under the table. Creating a hideaway space can help you to relax when you need some time to yourself. It can help to calm your body and your mind. Relaxing can feel good, especially if you have had a busy and stressful day. It's kind of like camping. When we go away and stay in a tent outdoors, it's quiet, and you can hear the birds and sometimes the sea.

**ACTION**: What would your hideaway look like at home if you could create one? Finish this doodle by adding your ideas for a hideaway. What other colours, shapes and patterns would you like to add?

33

# Jar of Tears

Crying is normal. Our bodies are like rain jars. Sometimes we fill up with tears and we start to overflow. It can help to think of tears as little drops of feelings leaving your body. Everyone cries and sometimes we can feel much better after letting it all out.

**ACTION**: What makes you feel sad? What causes your jar to overflow? If you need some space to cry or to let it all out, then this doodle can help you. Finish the doodle with colours, patterns, shapes and anything else that you want to add. When you are finished, would you like to share this with someone? Who could you share this with?

**34**

# Tunes On

Songs are really powerful! Are there songs that help you to feel happy? Are there songs that help you to feel energized? Are there songs that help you to feel other emotions? Songs help to create feelings and emotions in us. Sometimes music is a way for us to let our emotions out.

**ACTION**: What music do you like to listen to? If you were to write a song about how you are feeling right now, what would the title be? Complete this doodle with any other colours, shapes or patterns that you want to add.

**35**

# The Wishing Lamp

Imagine finding a lamp that could grant your wishes. What would you wish for? How would you feel if those wishes came true? Would any of those wishes help you with something that you are worrying about right now? Imagine that there is no limit to the amount of wishes that this lamp could help make come true for you. You could have as many as you like.

**ACTION**: Fill this doodle with wishes. What would you wish for? Don't forget to add any colours, patterns and shapes that you want to on your doodle.

**36**

# Flying Note

Have you ever made a paper plane and sent a flying note to someone? Is there someone on your mind you would like to share something with? Sometimes sharing just one thing can make all the difference to feeling lighter and worry free. This is because when we keep something on our minds and don't share it, it can sometimes feel like it's stuck on replay.

**ACTION**: Would you like to share something with someone? Add your message to this doodle and finish it with colours, shapes and patterns. Maybe you could take a picture of it and send it to someone.

**37**

# Time to Talk

Sometimes we don't say what we really want to because we are worried about what someone else might think or do. These things that we don't say can feel like heavy weights on our mind and they can cause us to feel really hurt, annoyed, frustrated or even angry at times. Is there something on your mind that you really want to say?

**ACTION**: This is your space to say whatever you want. Fill the speech bubble with words. Let go of all of the things that you want to express. Notice how you feel. Keep adding colours, patterns and doodles to this paper.

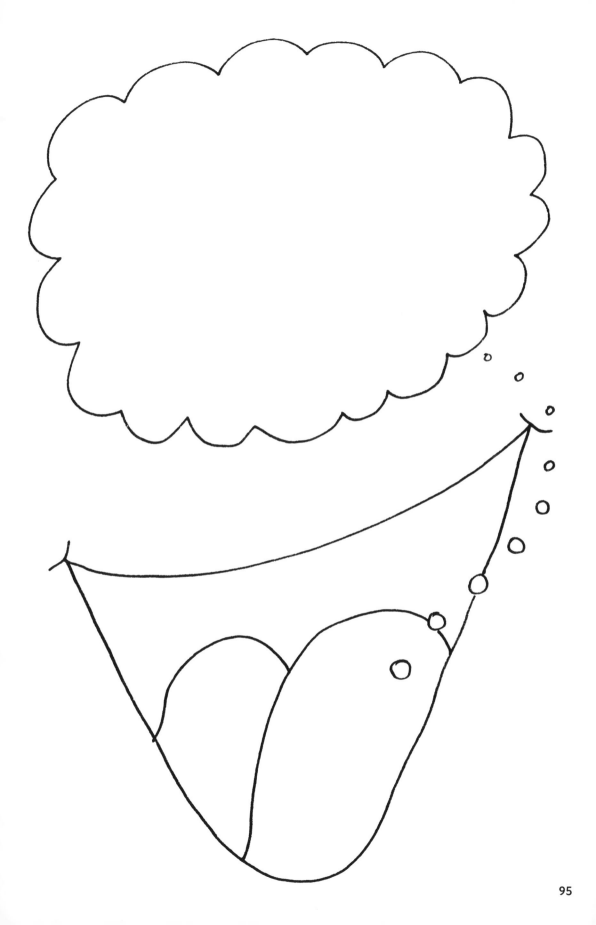

## 38

# The Compass

Sometimes we have to make a decision that worries us because we don't know what to decide. We don't know which way to go. Like when we get to a restaurant and don't know what to order because we want more than one thing. Sometimes our worries can have more than one way to be solved. This compass doodle can help you to decide which way to start.

**ACTION**: Think about a worry that you are having and write down the different ways that you can help your worry to stop playing over and over in your head. Choose where to start by adding the hands to the dial. Starting with one way doesn't mean that you can't go back to other ways too; it's just helpful to have a place to start. Finish the doodle by adding your own shapes, patterns and colours too.

**39**

# Stars and Planets

Imagine that the people you think about the most in your world are stars and planets. Stars and planets can be magical and beautiful. They can also be mysterious and adventurous. Some planets are ice-cold, and some are on fire. Imagine that you could create new stars and planets and name them.

**ACTION**: Who do you think about the most? Doodle new stars and planets for them. What colours, shapes, patterns and names would they have? What other shapes or things will you add to your doodle?

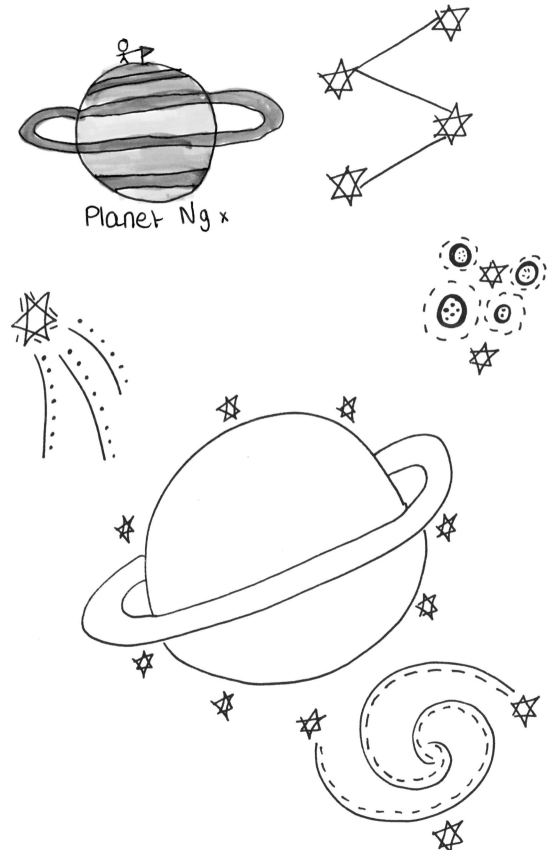

Planet Ng x

# 40

# Growing Kindness

Did you know that scientists have proven that kindness is good for you? When you are kind to yourself or others, it helps your own brain and body to be healthy, happy and smart. This is because when we are kind to others, this can release more feel-good chemicals in our brain which helps our whole body to feel strong. When we are kind to others it can help them to feel good too, although the most important person to be kind to is yourself.

**ACTION**: Finish this doodle with lots of kind thoughts towards yourself and other people. Notice how you feel when you are kind towards yourself and others. You are growing a kindness plant!

41

# Angels

This doodle is all about the people in your life who are helpful and kind towards you and others, the people who are like angels. They are caring and thoughtful, and if you need to ask for help, they are the ones you feel safe to talk to.

**ACTION**: Who are the angels in your life? Complete this doodle with words, colours, patterns, pictures or anything else that you want to.

## 42

# My Online World

Do you like to spend time online? What do you like doing and who do you like to talk to? Are there people you don't like to talk to, and why? Do you feel safe online? Do you worry about anything? This doodle can help you to celebrate what you love about being online, and it can also help you to talk about the things that worry you online.

**ACTION**: Complete the doodle to create your online world, adding all of the things that you like to do and the things that worry you too, maybe also adding people, places, games, websites, chatrooms and anything else that you want to.

## 43

# Balancing Act

Have you got something on your mind? What do you need help with the most right now? If you are worrying about a few things, you could use this doodle to write them down on the rocks. Some rocks are bigger than others, just like some worries are bigger than others. How big are your worries? Are there enough rocks? Do you need to add more?

**ACTION**: Once you add your doodles and your worries to the rocks, you can circle the ones that feel the biggest. Now you've created a list. Do you need to talk to anyone about what's on your list?

## 44

# Up, Up and Away

This balloon will take you to see anyone you want to in the world. Is there someone or more than one person you are missing? Where would you go to visit them? What would you say or do? You can also take anyone you want to with you. Do you want to take a person or a pet with you?

**ACTION**: Add all of the people you might take with you. Write the names of the people you want to visit in the clouds. Would you like to add anything more to the doodle, like colours, shapes and patterns? Maybe even photos?

## 45

# Celebrate You

Do you ever celebrate yourself? It's important to pat yourself on the back and remind yourself how well you are doing. Being your own best cheerleader can help you to feel healthy and happy. It helps you to be confident and to try new things because you know that you are strong enough to do amazing things. The more you can congratulate yourself, the more confident you can be. This doodle is a celebration of you!

**ACTION**: You are going to need some other people to help you with this. There are six speech bubbles. Ask people you care about to fill these speech bubbles with words that celebrate you, adding words that show just how amazing you are. Complete this doodle with colours, shapes and patterns. Maybe you could take a photo and keep it somewhere to remind yourself how awesome you are!

**46**

# Heart Wishes

What does your heart wish for most right now that won't cost money? Take some nice relaxing breaths and close your eyes. Place your hand on your heart and ask your heart, what do you wish for most right now? What thoughts come to you first? Imagine that you could wish for anything and your heart knows what it wants most.

**ACTION**: Fill this doodle with your heart wishes. Fill it with colours, shapes, patterns, words and anything else you would like to. What does it feel like to look at all of these things that you are wishing for?

## 47

# Switching Off

Our computers need to switch off sometimes and rest, just like our brains. Our brains need rest at night so that we can be healthy and strong. Sometimes it can be hard if you have lots of worries on your mind. This doodle is a space to think of as many things as you can to help you to switch off at night, things like talking to someone before you go to bed to help you to let go of some worries, or maybe putting on some relaxing music, having a weighted blanket or reading.

**ACTION**: What are the things that help you to switch off at night? How do you get ready for bed and sleep? Is there anything that you need help with? Fill this page with lots of ways to get a restful sleep.

## 48

# Hug in a Mug

Do you ever feel like you need a big hug in a mug? Like a hot chocolate with all the cream and the marshmallows and biscuits? It's nice to treat ourselves sometimes, and treating ourselves can help us to feel good. Sometimes when we are worrying about something, treating ourselves kindly can help us to reset, like a computer that needs to reboot.

**ACTION**: What would you add to your 'hug in a mug' to help you to reset or start fresh? Finish the doodle with lots of awesome extras. Doodle away!

## 49

# Bin It

Have you finished worrying about something? Is there something on your mind that you don't want to worry about anymore? It can feel good to throw away the worries that we do not want to keep thinking about, especially if we don't need to worry about them anymore. This bin loves to eat worries.

**ACTION**: What would you like to throw in the worry bin today? What don't you want to keep on your mind? Is there anything else that you want to add to this worry bin?

**50**

# Diamond

A diamond is a precious stone because each one is unique. Diamonds shine brightly in the world. They reflect all the colours around them and they are strong. To become a diamond, they have to go through lots of pressure. Just like you, there will never be the exact same diamond in the world. Next time you feel like you are not shining, remember that you are unique and strong. You are exactly who you are meant to be, and you are amazing!

**ACTION**: Complete this diamond doodle any way that you want! Add any colours, words, shapes or anything else that's important to you!

# AFTERWORD

I hope that you have loved doodling your worries away and that you have enjoyed taking some time to be creative. When I doodled this book for you, I created a corner in my house where I could go to be creative. It's a comfortable space with big pillows, by a window for sunny fresh air and lots of places around me to store creative materials like pens, paints and pencils. This is also my go-to safe place when I want to relax and take some time just to think for myself. Having a creative corner somewhere can really help you to be more relaxed when you are being creative and we know that being creative can really help us when we feel anxious or worried about anything because it's a great way to take a break from worrying and can often help us to solve our problems too.

So now that you are being more and more creative and you are finding your creative spark, I hope that I can inspire you to keep being creative and grow your *bouncebackability* (how you bounce back up when feeling down) from worrying or anxious times.

You could maybe try different ways to be creative to find what helps you even more, like:

- Painting your anxiety colours with acrylics, watercolours or paint pens on canvas or paper.

- Creating collages about how you feel from cut-out magazines or images from the internet and you can do this virtually on your computer too.

- Colouring-in books with shapes, animals and themes that you like.

- Learning a new instrument like the guitar or drums.

The most important thing is to keep talking about how you are feeling and, if you need some extra help, then there are also other places online where you can find help to talk about your anxiety and worrying, like: www.youngminds.org.uk and www.themix.org uk.

Keep on creating!

*Tanja Sharpe*

www.tanjasharpe.com